Trixie's Summer

Story by Heather Hammonds   Illustrations by Claire Bridge

Trixie was a little white mouse
who lived in a cage
in Bridget's classroom.

On the last day of school,
Miss Andrews asked,
"Who would like to take Trixie home
for the summer?
I promised to let James do it,
but now he is sick."

Bridget really wanted
to take care of Trixie.
"I'll do it," she said.

"Thank you, Bridget," said Miss Andrews.

"Your mom might not let you," whispered Bridget's friend Erin.

"I'll keep Trixie in my bedroom and tell Mom about her later," said Bridget. "I don't think she'll mind."

After school, the girls carried Trixie to Bridget's house.
Bridget peered under the cloth that covered Trixie's cage.

"Trixie is very cute," she said. "I wish I could keep her forever."

When they got home,
Bridget filled Trixie's water bowl.
Then she hid the cage
inside the closet in her bedroom.

"When are you going to tell your mom about Trixie?" asked Erin.

"Oh ... I'll do it later," said Bridget, who was starting to feel guilty. She knew that she really should have checked with Mom first.

5

When Erin had gone home,
Bridget decided that it was time
to show Trixie to Mom.
But when she opened the door
of her closet,
she saw that the cage was empty.
Trixie had disappeared!

"Oh, no!" she cried. "She's escaped!
I must have left the door of the cage open."

Bridget hunted for Trixie,
but she couldn't find her anywhere.
She was very worried
about the little mouse.

Then she had a thought.
Perhaps Trixie was hungry,
and ran into the kitchen
because she could smell food there.

Bridget tiptoed along the hallway,
toward the kitchen.
She could see Mom in the living room.

Bridget crawled around the kitchen
on her hands and knees.
"Trixie," she whispered, "where are you?"

Just then, Bridget's cat Tiger
rubbed against her legs
and meowed loudly.
Bridget jumped in fright!

Tiger sniffed around on the floor
and began to look excited.

Bridget guessed
that Tiger could smell Trixie.
She crawled behind him
as he sniffed under the kitchen table.

Then Tiger crouched down
beside the broom closet.

"What **are** you doing?" asked Mom, as she came into the kitchen.

"We're trying to find Trixie," said Bridget. "I was going to tell you about her, but then she escaped."

So Bridget told Mom
all about the mouse.
"I'm sorry I brought Trixie home
without asking you first.
But no one else could look after her
during the summer."

Mom frowned.
"We'd better find that mouse
before Tiger catches her," she said.

"I think she must be in the broom closet,"
said Bridget, "because Tiger is trying
to get his paw under the door."

"I'll put Tiger outside," said Mom.

When Mom came back,
she opened the broom closet door
very slowly and quietly.

Bridget peered around it, and said,
"I can see Trixie.
She's in that bucket and she can't get out!
Look, she's running around and around!"

"Quick!" said Mom.
"I'll throw this cloth over the bucket.
Run and get the cage."

Bridget brought the cage to the kitchen. Then, very carefully, she reached down into the bucket and picked Trixie up. She put her back into the cage and shut the door.

"Mom, please can Trixie stay?" begged Bridget.
"It's just for the summer."

Mom nodded and said,
"I quite like pet mice.
Perhaps Trixie would like some toys
to keep her busy in her cage."

"We could go to the pet store
and buy some for her," said Bridget.

"Good idea," said Mom. "But before we go,
we'd better put the cage on a high shelf.
We shouldn't let Tiger catch Trixie."

Later that day,
Bridget and Mom watched the little mouse running inside a new exercise wheel.

"I think Trixie is going to have a really good summer with us," laughed Bridget.